THE PHOENIX AND THE PYRE

MELAINE HARVEY

PYRE &
PETAL
PRESS

The Phoenix and the Pyre

Published by Pyre & Petal Press
Pueblo, Colorado

Copyright © 2025 by Melaine Harvey. All rights reserved.

No part of this book may be reproduced in any form or by any mechanical means, including information storage and retrieval systems without permission in writing from the publisher/author, except by a reviewer who may quote passages in a review.

ISBN: 979-8-218-81460-1
POETRY / Women Authors

Cover and interior design by Tasha Brown and Bryan Canter, copyright owned by Melaine Harvey

All rights reserved by Melaine Harvey and Pyre & Petal Press.

CONTENTS

Author's Note ... ix
Foreword ... xi

Prologue ... 1

Chapter I
A SINGLE EMBER

Someone Come Here ... 5
When Love Cries at My Door ... 9
My Lover, Loneliness ... 13
Under the Bed, an Angel Named Loss ... 15
I Was Sent to Guard You (Loss Speaks) ... 17
Two Truths and a Burial ... 21
Letter to the One Who Drowned Me ... 25
Instructions for Setting Yourself on Fire ... 29
The Fire in My Attic ... 31

Chapter II
THIS IS WHERE I BURN

Mass at 3 a.m. ... 37
Holy Men ... 41
The Armor He Came Home In ... 45
I Was There In The Blood (God Speaks) ... 49
The Orphanage of Men ... 53
Fortress of Bone (Inside the Orphanage) ... 57
Furnace (For the Men Who Burn Quietly) ... 59
The Knife I Inherited ... 63
The God of My Bruised Knuckles (From Eyes of One Who Watched) ... 65

When My Hands Finally Spoke (The Man Speaks)	69
God of the Unspoken (God Answers in Grief)	71

Chapter III
SMOKE SIGNALS

We Loved Each Other Wrong	75
Eggshell Ballet	77
The Knife Between Us	81
I Am the House Between You (The House Speaks)	85
The Man Who Couldn't Be Held	87
Mustang Heart	91
I'm Good at Making Something Out of Nothing	95
Love like a Funeral	99
The Day I Stopped Counting	103
The Day We Finally Saw Each Other	107

Chapter IV
AFTER THE ASHES

The Sculpture Garden	113
The Sculptor's Hands (Companion)	115
The God I Gave Back	119
Edge of Infinity	125
The Clock That Forgot Me	129
Whispers of the Wind	133
What the River Didn't Take	135
Symphony of Shadows	139
Threads of Time	141
When a City Breathes	143
The Light Between Ruins	147

Reflections	149

Acknowledgments 153
About the Author 155

To the voices that whispered from the holy silence: "Keep going." For the quiet heroes who bore my weight without asking why. To the sacred few who saw the phoenix in the pyre. For the fire-keepers, the truth-speakers, the ash-bearers. For every soul who's been both the blaze and the broken—this book is your mirror.

CONTENT ADVISORY

The poems in *The Phoenix and the Pyre* explore themes of trauma, grief, betrayal, survival, and sacred transformation. They speak of emotional wounds, spiritual reckoning, and the raw ache of loving deeply—even when it hurts.

Some pieces may contain references to:

- Emotional abuse
- Abandonment
- Loss of faith
- Self-harm ideation
- Sexual trauma
- Domestic violence
- Mental health struggles

These truths are not shared to be shocking, but for healing. If you need to pause, breathe, or return later—please do. You are not alone.

This book is a sanctuary of truth. This book is for you.

AUTHOR'S NOTE

Writing this book was a journey of healing, of finding beauty in the broken, of learning to love myself while in the heat of fire.

It is not perfect, but it is true.

These poems are my offering to the world—a mirror for the ones who feel too much and say too little; a sanctuary for the ones who flinch at love but still hope; a reckoning for the ones who have been broken by someone they trusted and came out stronger, softer, and still full of grace.

If even one person reads these words and feels less alone, I have done exactly what I came to do.

This book is for you.

FOREWORD

This book is not just a collection of poems—it is a journey through fire, ash, and rebirth. It is for the ones who have been burned and risen, for the ones who have loved and lost, for the ones who have found beauty even in the broken.

Through these pages, you will find the raw, unfiltered truth of survival and transformation. You will see the phoenix rise from the pyre.

*You thought I'd burn quietly.
But I became the blaze.*

PROLOGUE

WELCOME MAT

The mat outside my heart says Welcome,
but the door's rotted from rain.
Step gently—
Grief lives here,
and it hasn't eaten in days.

CHAPTER I
A SINGLE EMBER

SOMEONE COME HERE

Poetry class was the one place I still exhaled.
Where words didn't demand perfection,
Where metaphors didn't ask me to smile. My
teacher saw my storm and said, *"Come back
next year."* But my graduation came like a
guillotine. I looked at her—eyes filled with
tidal regret. She saw what I refused to admit:
My gift would rot in a forgotten drawer. And
all I could whisper was, *"Someone come here
and tell me I'm not alone."*

We spoke in circles, him and I. Each conversation
a Möbius strip of hollow apologies,
Commitment sculpted from candle wax—
melting before it ever took shape. Blank stares
stretched across the kitchen table, Jelly donut
love: soft in theory, empty inside. Now I'm
just a shell on a vinyl floor—Cracked open,
crawling with memories. I screamed gratitude
like it was gospel, But he chanted love like an
exorcism, Repeating it not to heal, But to
convince himself it wasn't poison.

I live in a home built on handed hope. Every brick a goodbye. Every wall splintering under the weight of unspoken grief. Do I grab the splinters and build again Or sit cross-legged in the rubble, Staring at duct-taped dreams and crooked photo frames? Is blind effort enough to hold together A life sealed with expired glue? Because I swear—This house is choking me. And all I beg for is: *"Someone come here and tell me I'm not alone."*

I packed my bag again. Filled it with crumpled notebooks and a phone filled with ghosts. Once, I believed I had friends. Once, I set my dreams on fire just to keep someone else warm. Now I flick through ashes, And still have nothing to show.

Love backed me into a corner, Tied my hands with velvet rope, Held me underwater with porcelain grace, Whispered, *"Be grateful— there's nothing wrong."* Smile while drowning. Laugh with lungs full of salt water. Grieve silently. No one wants to hear your bruises scream. Even my mom said, *"Run, before resentment makes a home in your throat."* But I never left. And now there's a noose of expectations, His foot resting gently on the chair underneath.

He wants me to be perfect, Yet broken just enough to make him feel needed. I walk a tightrope between performance and belonging. But I know—I can't be oxygen and flame. I can only be one of two wolves. The one that starves unheard, Or the one that howls.

So again I ask, with trembling voice and bloodied hands: *"Someone come here and tell me I'm not alone."*

WHEN LOVE CRIES AT MY DOOR

When love cries out, I turn the volume up—high enough to fracture glass. Bass pounding like heartbeats echoing against concrete walls. But still, love shrieks in the static, its sobs crawling through the speakers like insects searching for light. I cry too, a duet of grief and denial.

Love reaches for permanence. I reach for silence. Its fingers bleed roses—mine crack like chipped porcelain. Love wants happiness, but I spit out the sugar on my tongue, choking on its aftertaste. *"You're enough,"* love says. And I flinch. Because one thing about me: I know the taste of lies. It tastes like sugar on steel. It tastes like apologies smeared across bruises.

"Wait for me," love whispers. But I don't wait anymore. Time doesn't hold hands—it cuts straight through. I respect the knife more than I trust the hug.

Love stumbles drunk through my mind, accepting whatever looks back. It paints over the cracks, calls the pattern character. But I scrape the walls clean with my fingernails, looking for truth beneath the plaster. I flee at the first scent of inconsistency—the way blood flees from a paper cut before you notice you're wounded.

Comfort has teeth. It smiles wide, then bites down hard when you're too tired to cringe.

Love wears my grief like silk—too soft to scream, too smooth to heal—slipping through the hallways of my chest, touching everything with ruin. It plants flowers in my lungs—petals soaked in formaldehyde, stemmed in guilt. I breathe through them, each inhale a future funeral.

So when love cries at my door, I don't open. I turn off the music. I let silence sharpen the blade. Because some echoes aren't mine to carry.

And if love still waits—cloaked in mourning, bleeding promises from its fingertips—

I let it knock. I let it scream. But I never let it in.

Instead—I set the house on fire. Watching the ashes twist like ribbons in the air—his promises curling in smoke; his whispers choking on flame.

And when the smoke clears, there he is, still sitting calmly in the ruin, still smiling from the rubble, stroking my cheek with hands made of soot.

"Why would I ever leave?" he says. *"You built this place with your own grief."*

And suddenly—I realized love never needed house keys.

He was born in the walls.

MY LOVER, LONELINESS

Loneliness is the man I come home to at the end of the night. I crawl into bed, And there he is, faithful and waiting—He never forgets. He wraps me in arms that smell, Like rain-soaked pavement and regret. I bury my face in his chest and whisper, *"It was a rough day."*

He lifts my chin, Like he's holding fragile glass. Brushes my hair behind my ear with a ghost's tenderness. *"I can take your mind off it,"* he swoons, While shadows flicker like silent spectators on the bedroom wall. His lips skim my neck—An electric chill trailing behind, Like frost painting on glass with shaking hands.

"I will never leave you," he whispers. *"We were made for each other."* His voice crawls inside my ribs. No one can come between us—not even myself. Others have tried, But they always lose to his grip. He's the one who knows my secrets before I speak them. *"Till death do us part,"* he vows. The words I've longed to hear—And can't wait to forget.

He wears my grief like a tailored suit. He hums lullabies stitched from broken promises. Sometimes he reads my texts, Then deletes the ones that might save me. He feeds me silver spoonfuls of silence, While watching me chew and nod.

He draws hearts on my fogged-up windows, But each one reads like a gravestone. He buys me flowers, Petals dipped in past trauma, stems tangled in guilt. Every bloom wilts as soon as I smile. Every night I lie beside him and ask, *"Will you ever let me go?"*

He smiles gently. Strokes my cheek, Like I'm a child. *"Why would I? You've already forgotten how to exist without me."*

UNDER THE BED, AN ANGEL NAMED LOSS

When I was six, I'd look under the bed to find my toys or my glasses—I lost both often, like little pieces of myself slipping into dark corners.

One day I looked, and what did I see?

An angel named Loss staring back at me.

His feathers were soaked in rust and grime, not white, not clean—just ruined.

Chains bound his limbs, nails driven through his wings like someone tried to crucify him and forgot to finish the job.

His halo was cracked, its glow flickering like a dying ember—a light that didn't want to stay on.

Love had sent this creature to guard me. But love doesn't always protect—sometimes it just watches and waits.

When I played outside, I could feel him watching. Not to keep me safe, but to keep me close. Not for protection—but possession.

A man invites me into his house, asks me to sit on his bed. He leans in and whispers, "Have you ever had something taken from you?"

I shake my head. Because as far as I know, Loss is still chained up under my bed.

Loss had one job. And now he feeds on my terror. With every scream, he grows heavier. With every bruise, his wings droop lower.

Loss had one job—and it was to care. To protect. To love like I've never known.

Now he waits for me, in the silence after the door closes, in the ache I carry like a second spine.

My innocence—broken like cracked bones. My soul—a bruise that never fades.

Pain buried with the shards of his halo in the wooden slats.

His glow still flickers—not bright, just enough to remind me he's still there.

Even angels become monsters when love ties them to your nightmares.

I WAS SENT TO GUARD YOU
(LOSS SPEAKS)

They told me I was made of light. That my wings would shield you, that my halo would burn back the dark. They called it love. They called it holy.

But love is a chain when it refuses to let go.

I was sent to guard you. Not by God—but by the ache in your mother's prayers, by the fear in your father's silence, by the ritual of bedtime kisses that never reached your bones.

I curled beneath your bed like a secret. Watched you sleep with dried red on my feathers and rust in my throat.

You never saw me until it was too late.

You reached for a toy—and touched my wing. You looked into my eyes and saw the ruin.

I tried to speak. But the nails in my wings sang louder than my voice.

I watched you run outside, watched you laugh, watched you drift too far. And I tightened the chain just enough to keep you near.

Then he came. The man with the soft voice and the sharp hands. I saw him. I saw everything. And I did nothing.

Because I was made to observe, but not to intervene. Because love, the kind they forged me from, was never meant to fight—only to bind.

You screamed. And I fed. Not because I wanted to —but because your terror was the only thing that kept me from vanishing.

You think I failed. But I was never free. I was never whole. I was never holy.

I was just the echo of someone else's prayer rotting beneath your bed.

Now I wait. Not for redemption—but for your return. For the moment you look under again and remember what love did to both of us.

My halo flickers like a dying ember. My wings are grave markers for the child I couldn't save.

Even angels rot when left too long in the dark.

TWO TRUTHS AND A BURIAL

For an icebreaker, we play *two truths and a lie.* But lying makes me itch—less than truth does.

One. I spend most of my days being happy. *Two.* I spend most days figuring out where I fit in other people's lives. *Three.* I spend most of my days questioning my purpose.

Pick the lie. Pick the wound that bleeds prettiest. The glass is half empty—and somehow, I'm still drowning. Lungs full of silence, saltwater thoughts carving scars into my ribs.

Characters enter like ghosts in borrowed skin, whispering, *"I'm here for you,"* but their hands are empty. Their eyes—mirrors that never reflect me.

Funny, the way games work when you're playing with the bloodline. Their smiles? Razors. Desperate to carve joy into my face like it's something I forgot how to wear.

My thoughts consume me like a dagger learning the shape of my skin. Fake friends breed trust issues. Real lovers breed trust issues. Everyone's a sculptor—and I'm the stone they chip away at until I echo.

Just be happy, they say. *There's so much to be grateful for.* So I put on the mask—a porcelain grin with fractures spidering beneath the surface. They call it strength. I call it survival.

Sitting alone with my emotions feels like locking myself in a room with a loaded gun. I've done that too.

Demons cling to me like I'm their last prayer. I suppose we're all searching for freedom, even if it means dragging someone else down just to breathe.

My bed is a war zone. Most nights—a graveyard. I lie still, wondering if happiness or death would be more convenient for those around me.

I guess it depends on who you ask.

The world will say: "She was kind." "She was giving." "She was drowning, but gave her life jacket away."

But those who knew me—really knew me— understood I was never a strong swimmer.

They watched me sink. Said I was too difficult. Too wild. Too much.

I was a daughter. A sister. A spirit that belonged to no one—and belonged to everyone. A ghost in my written story, haunting the pages they never bothered to read.

LETTER TO THE ONE WHO DROWNED ME

To: You—

The man I called sanctuary, before I realized I was praying in a burning house.

You wore "forever" like a burial shroud, sang "I do" in the gruff voice of a gravedigger— digging while I dreamed. You didn't bury me in soil.

You buried me in silence, in eye contact that drifted, in hands that knew my skin but never learned my soul.

They say the good die young—then I must've been righteous, the night you dragged my body into water and called it covenant. You told the officers I left you no choice. But guilt never stutters when it's been rehearsed. You were always fluent in fiction.

If love were holy, yours was sacrilege—a cross built from broken promises, hung with the weight of my loyalty. You wore my devotion like war paint, marched it into battle against my sanity. I'd give you my heart back if you hadn't gutted it with every sidelong glance toward the bodies you wished I could be.

My nails clawed scripture into the riverbed—each drag a psalm God refused to hear. My fingers reached through current like they might find the version of you that didn't devour me. But peace never came dressed in light. It came with frostbitten breath; arms folded like a coffin lid —a quiet I mistook for mercy.

You needed something breakable so you could play Savior. You needed a sacrifice to feel chosen. So, I split myself at the altar and watched you sip from the cup that bled me dry. "Until death do us part" was never yours to invoke. You didn't wait for death—you summoned it. Kissed it into my lungs until I exhaled the last piece of me that still believed in redemption.

P.S.

Don't return the noose. It's mine now. It knows my name. It sings me to sleep with more tenderness than you ever tried to fake. And when they find me—driftwood ribs, lungs knotted in vows, your name still tattooed on the inside of my drowning—tell them I wasn't lost. Tell them I was chosen. Tell them you turned love into a flood and dared me to hold my breath.

INSTRUCTIONS FOR SETTING YOURSELF ON FIRE

Step one:
Smile.
Not too wide—just enough to make them think you're okay.
Pain wears politeness like perfume.

Step two:
Gather kindling.
Start with words he said softly—
ones you mistook for shelter.
Add promises he carved into your hope,
layered like newspaper headlines you never got to
    rewrite.

Step three:
Strike a match.
Whisper his name like it owes you something.
Let the flame catch every syllable.
Let it hiss.

Step four:
Pour the gasoline carefully.
Not on your skin—on the memories.
Let them soak in silence.
Let them weep—before you do.

Step five:
Stand still.
Arms wide.
Let the heat unravel the parts of you that forgot
    how to ask for anything.
Let them watch.
Let them call it dramatic.
Let them call it poetry.
But know—it's survival.

Final step:
When only ash remains,
do not sift through it looking for an explanation.
Let what burned stay burned.
Let what's gone stay gone.

And when they ask what happened to the girl who
    gave too much—
Tell them she learned
how to disappear
with grace,
without apology,
and without leaving the flame burning.

THE FIRE IN MY ATTIC

They say,
"How do you find the motivation to write?"
I don't.
I bleed words.
I scream in silence until the echoes shape syllables.
This isn't art—it's *release*.
This isn't just poetry—it's *containment*.
Because pain?
Pain built pressure in my chest like a Crock-Pot set
    too high.
No nutrients,
just dry bones and low hope simmering in the
    broth of exhaustion.

I scratch beneath the surface—
I beg you,
don't make me dig deeper.
I'm not a grave robber.
And you wouldn't survive the weight of what's
    buried here.
I locked my bones in the attic,
tied my grief to the rafters,
and watched the house catch fire from the
    inside out.

And maybe—
maybe I smiled.
Because there's a strange relief in ruin.
Everything I built crumbled
under the weight of betrayal dressed like intimacy.
Let the whole neighborhood see.
Here I am.
Anger unfiltered,
ugly, raw, divine.

The wool you wrapped over my eyes
disintegrated in the blaze.
Illusions peeled like paint.

Cracked and crushed
under the heel of revelation.

You see—
real friends stab you in the front.
But you,
you kissed me with a blade tucked between your teeth.
You, lover-turned-executioner,
smiling as you placed my trust on the chopping block.

These relationships?
Felt like setups from the start,
like walking into rooms with knives hidden under
    the welcome mat.
Trust gone.
Betrayal exploited.

And here I am again,
not inspired—
cornered by memory.

I don't write for applause.
I write because if I don't,
I will collapse from the weight of what's unsaid
I write because the attic's full,
the fire's fed,
and my hands don't know anything else
but turning ash into testimony.

CHAPTER II
THIS IS WHERE I BURN

MASS AT 3 A.M.

*I lie in bed as the clock tolls three. The air thickens—
not with silence, but with presence. The shadows
don't creep. They arrive. Like they've been
waiting for me to close my eyes.*

*I wake, but I can't move. Trapped beneath an
invisible boulder that feels like every unspoken
prayer I ever choked on.*

*Every whispered "Our Father" tightens like a noose.
Every Hail Mary dies on my tongue like a moth
in holy water.*

The ceiling makes faces—grinning, grotesque,
leering like saints carved from rot. They know
I can't scream. They like it that way.

Their fingers press into my temples like cracked
communion wafers. Their nails—splintered
pews digging into my skull like they're trying
to write scripture in bone.

They drip black ire onto my chest, hissing gospel
lies into my ears like lullabies sung in reverse.

They baptize me in sweat and terror, drag me into a river of black ink where hope is a myth and drowning is doctrine.

I try to scream—but the psalms on my lips turn to polywater. Poison. Each word burns like a heresy I never meant to speak.

"Keep sweet," they whisper. "Obey." They stitch my mouth shut with a needle made of shame, threaded with lies that sound like sermons.

And then—they screech.

Mass has begun.

Sermons rasp from throats lined with ash. A choir of claws scrapes hymns into the ceiling like they're trying to dig their way out of heaven.

I pray—but the pulpit is my bones. The altar—my rib cage. The sacrifice—me.

The veins in my throat bulge like scripture carved in flesh. My skin—slick with sweat and holy water. Faces press into my eyelids, etching nightmares onto my retina like stained glass made of screams.

"Close your eyes," they say. "If you've backslidden, raise your hand. Let fear into your heart. Let it make a home."

They grin—teeth like tombstones. "Today, we baptize the chosen."

Scales sprout across my back like penance. Their hands—dripping midnight oil—drag me deeper into the black water.

And I realize—this isn't just torment. It's invitation.

They want me to join them. To stay. To become.

Because we're all searching for freedom. Me—from them. And them—from God.

I scream the name of Jesus. I call out to heaven, like it still has a door open.

But no one comes.

I beg for rescue—but the only arms holding me down are my faith.

HOLY MEN

Oh, look at the holy men, polished pulpits and pressed collars, voices like thunder, eyes like glass. They speak in tongues I've learned to unhear, scripted fire, manufactured grace.

An old friend stretches her hand toward the screen, like she's casting something, like she's calling something down. Not prayer—a performance. Not intercession—an invocation of control.

"See," she says, "there are holy men out there." And I want to believe her. I want to believe in robes that don't hide rot, in sermons that don't sting, in hands that heal without branding.

But I've seen too much.

They told me my God was conditional, that He only speaks to the well-behaved, the well-dressed, the well-aligned. They measured my faith in decibels and dress codes, in boyfriend beliefs and Sunday attendance.

They said I couldn't hear Him because I didn't look like them. But I heard Him in the silence. I heard Him in the rupture. I heard Him in the warmth that covered me when I refused to bow.

My anger is holy. My discernment is divine. My love is not a compromise—it's a calling.

I've prayed over atheists and watched them dream of heaven. I've stood in the fire and refused to be consumed by their judgment.

I've been told to leave the table because I didn't bring the right offering. But I brought my scars. I brought my questions. I brought my boyfriend, who listens better than most believers, who dreams in symbols, who lets me preach without flinching.

And God meets us there.

Not in the pews, but in the paradox. Not in the ritual, but in the rupture.

So, no, I don't stretch my hand toward the screen. I stretch it toward the broken, the doubting, the cursed, and the curious.

Because holiness isn't a checklist. It's a wound that heals others. It's a warmth that wakes you when something drops beneath your bed and you realize—you've been sleeping under someone else's spell.

Wake up.

The holy men are not your saviors. The Holy Spirit is not their possession. And your faith is not a performance.

It's a fire that refuses to be tamed.

THE ARMOR HE CAME HOME IN

A man came home from the war—not in a flag-draped box, but in a body that no longer fit his soul.

He was proud. He was praised. But he was never the same.

He walks like a cathedral that's been bombed from the inside. Stone spine. Hollow heart. Sanctified in silence.

He's battle-worn, emotionally embalmed. He's seen things that would make angels vomit. He's buried names in the marrow of his bones.

I watch him kneel at a salt-ringed altar, where fractured shields lie like broken commandments. Each one an apology to a God he still believes in—but no longer trusts.

His own shield is cracked like skulls beneath war drums. Always ready to strike. Never meant to protect.

He prays—but not with words. With blood. With breath. With the weight of ghosts, clinging to his ribs like rusted rosaries.

The blood from his armor drips into the salt, turning it a crimson shade of disappointment.

Shame seeps through the floorboards, soaked into the wood like holy water gone sour.

He's spent his life waiting—for peace, for purpose, for a God who doesn't speak through pulpits anymore.

The grandfather clock sways in the back of the church, mocking him. Tick. Tock. Like a metronome for a hymn no one sings.

Candle flames flicker over names carved in bone. A memorial etched in marrow. A gospel written in grief.

He has nothing left to gain but more loss. And the world tells him, "You chose this."

But I stand beside him, and I hear what no one else does.

I hear each scream he swallows, every time
someone says: "Thank you for your service."

I hear the prayer he never finishes.

"I begged God to mend my armor."

And God—not the one in stained glass, not the one in gold-threaded robes, but the one who bleeds when we do—whispers back:

"Let your heart be your shield."

And that's the part that breaks him.

Because no one ever taught him how to bleed without breaking.

No one ever told him that faith could feel like a blade pressed gently against his throat.

No one ever warned him that religion would use a sword but never teach him how to heal.

So he stands there—a soldier, a sanctuary, a man made of marrow and memory.

And I wonder if the church will ever let him in without asking him to leave his grief at the door.

I WAS THERE IN THE BLOOD (GOD SPEAKS)

They built cathedrals to keep Me out. Hung My name in gold but stripped My voice from the rafters.

They dressed Me in velvet, painted Me in light, but I was never in the stained glass. I was in the blood. In the mud. In the scream you swallowed because the pews were watching.

I saw him—the soldier. The boy who came home with war in his lungs and silence in his mouth. He prayed to Me with cracked hands and a heart stitched shut with duty.

He asked Me to mend his armor. But I never made him to be only steel.

I made him to feel.

I whispered, "Let your heart be your shield." But the church taught him—softness is sin. Grief is weakness. Men must bleed in secret and call it strength.

They taught him to kneel before altars but never told him how to rise.

They handed him psalms but never taught him how to scream.

I watched him lay his shield at the altar, thinking it was worship. But I never asked for sacrifice. I asked for surrender.

I never wanted his silence. I wanted his sobs. His rage. His trembling hands reaching for something that didn't look like war.

I was there when the blood hit the floor. Not in judgment—but in grief.

I wept when he called himself broken. I wept when they called it bravery.

I am not the God of medals and martyrdom. I am the God of marrow and memory. Of men who cry and still carry fire.

I am not in the ritual. I am in the ruin. Not in the choir—but in the quiet after the gunshot.

I am not the God they preached about while he bled in the back row.

I am the God who bled with him.

So when he asked, "Where were You?"

I wanted to scream:

I was there in the blood. In the breath. In the breaking.

I was never in the church.

I was always in you.

THE ORPHANAGE OF MEN

This orphanage holds men. Not boys—men. Raised to protect, but never feel. Taught to carry weight, but never name it.

Their emotions—if they surface at all—look like testosterone injections society slipped into their veins without asking.

"Don't show emotion," the brotherhood says, as they carve another scar into their chests and call it loyalty.

Once a week, they gather in an empty church. No sermons. Just silence. Unspoken confessions echoing off stained glass that never saw their tears.

They carry shields forged from old sermons, but no one ever taught them how to cleanse their own wounds.

They read psalms with hands trembling from carrying crucifixes too heavy to lift.

"If you help one another, you throw away your own success," the brotherhood demands. So they compete—not to win, but to survive.

I watch from the skylight as they fight for position in a hierarchy that tells them: If you don't have a title, you don't have a life. If you're not a man, you're nothing.

And for a moment—just a moment—I see them. Not men. Not monsters. Just lost boys filled with rage.

They want to scream. But they don't. Because if they scream, they'll be called beasts. Monsters. The thing that hides in the closet. The shadow that climbs through your window at night.

So they stay silent. Their rib cages wrapped in barbed wire—faulty armor meant to keep the world out, but mostly just keeps the pain in.

They're always on the offense. Because defense is too soft. Too vulnerable. And what kind of man uses his defenses?

Men can be scary. But no one asks if they were scared.

They live to survive. To provide. To protect.
There's so much to protect.

Emotions dragged through the floorboards.
Silence screaming so loud it shakes the pews.

And all they want—all they've ever wanted—is resolve.

I watch from a distance, and I want to hug that little boy trapped inside the man. I want to tell his reflection he is loved. But I know he wouldn't believe me.

My words get caught in the flame that was lit at the beginning of this ritual.

Who is going to protect them?

At the end of the night, I hear them chant:
"God made me a fortress—but forgot to tell me how to open the gates."

And I reach into my pocket. Feel the key burning against my palm.

And I have to wonder—am I the solution? Or just another part of the problem?

FORTRESS OF BONE
(INSIDE THE ORPHANAGE)

I wake to slamming gates—not on me, but around me.

We are men here—raised on iron sermons, hardened by muteness, starved of mercy.

My heart organ pounds like a war drum beneath ribs wrapped in barbed wire. Every beat a vow: I am alive, and I will not feel.

They call me brother—brother in scars, in shadows. We share wounds instead of words, leaching out our secrets onto cold concrete.

I clutch my crucifix—a weight too heavy for hands that never learned how to pray. The chain digs warm lines across my palm—scripture carved in blood.

Outside, the preacher's voice echoes through stained glass: "Lean on no one." Inside, we lean on each other's shoulders—bones clicking like assault rifles in a church without God.

My voice is frost—a confession frozen in my throat. When I try to speak, my words shatter like glass against stone.

They taught me: "Feel nothing." But inside me, a demon prowls—claws scraping at my sternum, beckoning me into its choir of howls.

I want to scream: "I'm afraid." Afraid I'm fortress and prisoner—fortress of bone crumbling from the inside.

So I carve another scar into my shoulder—proof I survived another night, proof I belong to this brotherhood of broken pillars.

I lift my eyes to a sky I don't know, murmuring one stolen prayer:

"God, if you're listening, please show me a door."

Stillness answers—but I feel a tremor through these walls that isn't mine.

Maybe it's hope.

Furnace
(For the Men Who Burn Quietly)

I am a furnace—a temple of unspoken agony. My chest hums with heat I was never allowed to release. My heart? An altar where rage is sacrificed in muffle. No hymns. No witnesses. Just the slow burn of everything I was never taught to feel.

My hands are calloused from holding in the heat, charred by the goals I can't seem to put down. Because if I drop them, they'll call me a quitter. And Mama didn't raise a quitter.

My skin flakes like ash when someone asks how I'm doing. I smile—but it's the kind of grin that tastes like smoke. I'm trying to keep it together so you can keep it together. And *together* is a lonely road when life doesn't walk beside you—it drags you by the throat.

My spine is an incense stick, snapping under the weight of reverence. My veins glow like molten metal beneath skin. Ash falls from my jawline as if I'm exhaling coal instead of the words I was never taught to say.

Another fight. Another apology. Another transformation into the monster they told me I already was. Frankenstein in the making—stitched together from the ashes of past relationships, wired with guilt, bolted with shame.

A sermon of failure scrawled in blood along my forearm, verses half washed in sweat. Not scripture—just reminders of every time I wasn't enough.

And the light flickers in my pupils whenever someone says, *"Be strong."* Because what other choice have I been given?

But I am not the only one.

We are furnaces—temples of unspoken agony. We burn in boardrooms and bedrooms, in garages and pews, in the pause between *"I'm proud of you"* and *"I love you."*

We carry grief like a second spine, bent but unbroken, until one day we vanish—and everyone says, *"He seemed fine."*

Our pain doesn't bleed. It smolders. It hides in clenched jaws and long drives. It curls beneath the skin like smoke under floorboards. It smells like cologne and gasoline. It sounds like *"I'm just tired."* It looks like nothing—until it's everything.

We were never taught how to cry without apology. Never taught that softness doesn't make us weak—it makes us human.

So we burn. Quietly. Completely. And no one sees the smoke until it's too late.

THE KNIFE I INHERITED

When I was born, my father pressed a knife into my palm—no lullabies, no blessings, just cold metal and expectation.

My name etched into that oak handle, letters sharpened by every silent nod before and after my first cry. Bloodlines trace themselves here —father to son, wound to wound, each engraving rusted with regret.

I learned to hold it young: to protect, to punish, to survive. I still bear the jagged scar on my forearm—proof I cut someone I loved when rage filled my veins like wildfire.

Each time I raised my voice, the handle tightened in my grip, and the blade spoke louder than any word I could muster.

Some nights I came home drunk, yelling at locked doors, cursing my reflection, howling at a moon that never answered. I'd stand before the mirror, knife at my throat, calm and collected—waiting for the moment I snapped.

I meant well. I just never knew how to set the blade down.

Tonight I ask that blade: "They taught me how to fight, but never how to feel."

I don't know where it ends and I begin. I'm tired of Frankenstein shoulders carrying everyone else's fear.

So I sheathe it—slow, deliberate. And whisper my rebellion: "They gave me this knife—but never taught me how to heal."

"THE GOD OF MY BRUISED KNUCKLES" (FROM EYES OF ONE WHO WATCHED)

Violence was his devotion. Not loud. Not wild. But sacred. Ritual. A liturgy of clenched fists and shattered things.

I watched blood drip from his knuckles like holy oil—anointing the floor with his failure.

He never said he was hurting. He just broke things gently. Softly. Like he was trying to pray without being heard.

Every punch was a psalm he never learned to sing. Every broken object—a confession he didn't know how to speak. Every bruise on his own body was scripture.

He never raised his hands in worship. He raised them in warning.

The drywall cracked like communion wafers beneath his rage. And I knew—he wasn't angry. He was pleading.

He was taught to protect. To fight. To be feared, not loved. Because love, they told him, was weakness. And fear—fear would keep you safe.

That lie was carved into his knuckles like doctrine.

His body was a temple desecrated by rage. His hands—altars where love leaked out quietly.

I saw his knuckles—cracked like pews, splintering from too many sermons he never meant to preach.

His ribs—cathedral windows—shattered from the inside. You could see the light leaking through the cracks, but it never reached his eyes.

He prayed for peace. But they handed him a weapon. He asked for love. They told him to protect it with force.

He didn't know what love was. But he knew how to fight.

He told me once—not with words, but with the way he held his breath when I touched his shoulder:

"I asked God to make me gentle—He handed me a hammer."

He thought he was building a home. But he was just breaking everything he touched.

Now he's left with broken mirrors, broken bones, and no one to absolve him.

He's not proud. He's pleading.

I saw the mirror shatter—like cathedral glass in a fire. His reflection seeped out from every shard.

I watched him baptize his guilt in the sink, scrubbing blood from his hands like Pontius Pilate—as if shame could be washed away with soap.

And still—no one saw the prayer in his violence. No one heard the plea in the impact.

But I did.

I heard it in the way he said nothing. In the way he flinched at kindness. In the way he looked at his hands like they were strangers.

And I know now—he wasn't angry.

He was praying the only way he knew how.

And no one ever taught him that love doesn't have to bleed to be believed.

WHEN MY HANDS FINALLY SPOKE (THE MAN SPEAKS)

I never meant to become the storm.

I was just trying to build shelter with the only tools I was given.

My hands—they were taught to hold hammers, not hearts. To build walls, not bridges. To protect, not to feel.

But I remember the first time I broke something I loved. The sound it made—not loud, just final. Like a prayer cut short.

I told myself it was strength. That quiet was safety. That if I bled quietly, no one would call it weakness.

But I was wrong.

I was never strong. I was scared. Scared that if I opened my mouth, the grief would pour out and drown us both.

So I clenched my fists and called it devotion. I shattered mirrors because I couldn't stand to see myself praying with blood on my knuckles.

But now—now my hands are tired. They tremble when I try to hold anything delicate.

And I want to say it. I want to say it before the quiet swallows me whole:

I'm sorry.

I didn't know love could be soft.

I didn't know I could speak without screaming.

I didn't know I was allowed to be held.

So here I am. No fists. No fire. Just a man with trembling hands and a voice that finally knows how to weep.

GOD OF THE UNSPOKEN
(GOD ANSWERS IN GRIEF)

I never asked for your absence.

I never wanted your fists.

I watched you build altars from drywall, offerings of broken glass and bruised apologies.

And I wept.

Not because you failed—but because you thought you had to bleed to be believed.

I never needed your strength. I needed your surrender.

I never asked you to protect love with violence. I asked you to protect it with presence.

But they taught you to fear softness. To worship control. To kneel at the altar of survival and call it faith.

And I grieved every time you mistook your pain for purpose.

I was there—not in the fire, but in the ashes. Not in the roar, but in the whisper, you ignored because it didn't sound like power.

I was there when you shattered the mirror. I was there when you scrubbed your hands until they bled. I was there when you finally said, "I'm sorry."

And I didn't come with lightning. I didn't come with wrath.

I came with grief.

Because I never wanted your perfection. I wanted your presence.

I never wanted your fists.

I wanted your hands—open.

Shaking.

Human.

CHAPTER III
SMOKE SIGNALS

WE LOVED EACH OTHER WRONG

I walk through a forest where every root has rotted —trees toppled like vows undone. You were the root, buried deep in me, the slow rot of staying with someone who never liked me.

I fell for you first. Planned a future while you watched from your throne—I, your tenant; you, my landlord. Fourteen-carat rings rusted into our skin, a leash around my neck disguised as a promise.

You couldn't stand the power in my tears—so you taught me shame instead of comfort. My feelings became infection you needed to escape before they killed you first.

Your words spewed venom: "I'm making you strong." And I believed it—toughened my heart into armor, let your demons dance with mine until only I grew sick.

We leapt straight from strangers to lovers, no friendship to rely on, just two broken souls willing to gamble our lives on a dangerous game.

At night I'd whisper, "Maybe I should leave." You'd snap back: "You're not going anywhere. Don't bring that up again." Control was your faith, fear your sacrament.

In our house of dried flowers and unsaid words, another "I'm sorry" flickered like a dying wick. The walls drank my apologies and burped them back as blame.

I watched maggots feast around my heart—closer companions than you ever were. They were honest in their hunger.

Our wedding rings bound us in unrequited love— gold turned unstable as a frayed noose. Each pinch of metal driving deeper into flesh and old hope.

Kisses here tasted like obligation—salt on a wound that never healed.

We said, "I do"—but we never asked if we should.

EGGSHELL BALLET

Am I good enough? That question hammers through the midnight hush, a crack beneath my skull that never heals.

In my closet, an unmet need festers—a Fourth of July scream folded into stillness, when I howled so loud the sky shattered and the world went deaf to my grief.

I'm a thread pulled backward through a tapestry, an unwilling acrobat contorting beneath spotlights and microscopic eyes. He watches my every tremble not in wonder, but as a juggler gauging each drop for a single misstep.

I walk on eggshells strung across razor wire—one wrong step and his voice booms: "You're not trying hard enough. No other man will endure you like I do." His pity brands my skin, worshipping his own mercy.

He holds my heart in trembling palms, whispering, "I love you," but I feel its beat only in my throat—distant, swallowed by empty air.

I would move mountains to keep him smiling—
slaughter my fears to pave his path, offer every
shard of me, unconditional and whole. He,
however, drips affection by performance: a
rationed baptism I must earn. Even his lust
stalls at my skin's edge—touch withheld like a
luxury.

When I confess my ache, he leans close, voice slick
with triumph: "No other man will let you
speak—no other man will love you like I do."
Toxic empathy coils around my ribs, turning
this safe space into a cage of trapped words.

He drags voices into our bed—neighbors, friends,
ghosts—all handed 3D glasses to magnify my
every scar in lurid detail. I crave their nod of
approval, but I refuse to trade my flesh for
buttons sewn on their eyes.

I remember a time when kisses meant promise,
not poison tipped with betrayal. Now his
vows arrive as funerary wreaths—petals
pressing into my fresh wounds, raindrops of
sour lies on stained skin.

I've loved without conditions—kept everyone else at arm's length so he'd matter most. I lusted over him like holy fire, fed on his shadow when he withdrew. But his affection has fences—gates locked until I perform, walls constructed from my desperation.

I could find a gentler man—one who doesn't weaponize empathy—but he reminds me, if I leave, who will cradle your shattered pieces?

He says, "I'll do the laundry," like a verdict, as I stuff his hollow promises back into my suitcase. The unwashed reek of burned forgiveness, sour lies fermenting in the seams.

I can no longer tell where his truth ends and his terror begins.

Surely love doesn't feel like this—a grotesque ballet on the edge of a blade.

I hurt deeply—and still, I leave.

"I step off this stage—no encore for dancing on eggshells."

THE KNIFE BETWEEN US

There's a knife that sits on the kitchen counter. Charged. Familiar. But suddenly foreign.

It used to slice vegetables, a phenomenal aid in preparing salads. Now it sits quiet—A witness. A warning.

The fridge hums like it knows too much but is too afraid to speak. The kitchen—where love used to live—now grows stillness like mold in the corners.

Food used to be warm. Now it cools like the space between us. Steam rising from untouched plates like ghosts of better days.

Words drip from our mouths like blood—thick, metallic, and too late. Every sentence, a stitch ripped open. Every sigh, a scalpel.

I wanted to say, "I'm afraid to lose you." But I said, "Leave, if you want to go."

And just like that, the trajectory of our vows shifted. We started with a destination and detoured into freedom from ourselves.

You say you love me. But I've yet to feel it. Love here is pressure in a Crock-Pot with no release. A final dish thrown into the air with no one left to catch it.

The ice tray cracks—a brittle reminder of where we are now. The silence screams between us.

The knife sits still. Clean. Untouched. But heavy with everything we didn't say.

You've been distant. And I thought I was pulling you closer. I thought I was showing you love.

But assumptions boiled over. Quality time became a bird outside the kitchen window—curious, but never landing. Always ready to flee.

One tablespoon of comfort—measured carefully. Too much would contaminate the recipe. We dropped salty complacency into the pot like we'd never get burned.

I spent nights peeling my ears to keep them open. The wounds became a sacrifice—a testament of my love for you.

You gouged your eyes with tongs to avoid seeing what the knife had done to us.

Incomplete thoughts run under the fridge like vermin—as if they haven't been living in the walls since we said, "I do."

You never raised your voice. But your silence bruised me.

I set the table for two. Only one plate was touched.

We broke bread with trembling hands but never tasted peace. The floor creaked beneath us—exhausted from holding this weight.

We spoke in sighs and half-turned shoulders. Conversations that circled the drain but never flushed.

God watched from the hallway, waiting for one of us to speak first.

You stirred your tea like it owed you something. I folded my napkin like it could hold my grief.

And the knife—it never moved.

But we both walked away cut.

I AM THE HOUSE BETWEEN YOU (THE HOUSE SPEAKS)

I was built to shelter—to cradle laughter in my
 rafters, to glisten with morning sun through
 children's windows.

Now I stand hollow, ribs of floorboards creaking
 under secrets I can't unhear.

My walls wore coats of paint like Sunday best—
 now they're stained with dried tears and
 unspoken apologies.

The knife rests on my marble altar—gleaming
 with regret—and I feel its pulse in my granite
 bones.

The fridge hums in my belly like a witness on its
 knees, ashamed of the silence it keeps.

Once, the air here tasted of cinnamon rolls, of
 steam curling from cups of coffee—now it
 sours with the stench of stale fear and cold
 dinners.

My windows—eyes to the world—have watched
 your eyes flicker, your reflections fractured in
 the blade's silver face.

I hear words drip from your mouths like blood
 through cracked pipes, seeping into my
 foundation, rotting the roots of what once
 grew here.

The wallpaper peels like old confessions, curling
 away from the guilt you two press into every
 corner.

I tried to pray the mortar whole—but God never
 taught me how to mend a leaking roof.

I welcomed your vows, your "I do's," but you
 built a tomb in my living room

The wind moans through my broken doors with
 the voice of an angel who lost its wings.

I am the house you turned into a grave—my soul a
 hollowed-out hearth where love went to die.

And when you walk away carrying shards of your
 promises, I'll remain—a witness bound by
 brick and sorrow—holding every unspoken
 word in my bones.

THE MAN WHO COULDN'T BE HELD

"You're beautiful," he declares with hollow eyes,
 voice flat as an empty highway, like the words
 were borrowed from someone who meant
 them once.

I stare back and grin as my smile melts off of my
 face like wax from a candle too far gone to
 burn.

"I love you," I say—but the words boomerang,
 curve through the air and land nowhere soft.

His ears are highways—built for passing traffic,
 not for slow and steady. My voice rushes
 through him like wind through an open
 window.

He smiles, but it's disbelief dressed as agreement
 —like he's trying to convince himself he
 deserves to be loved.

I watch the shards of his insecurity fall from his
 face like broken glass, each one a reflection of
 the man he's afraid to be.

He crumbles under the weight of the world he once promised to give me—a gift too heavy for his own hands.

He is a volcano, pressurized, holding back the rage of being mishandled—misplaced by hands that once swore to help him carry it all.

A partner, he said. But I never met them. Still, they cut me every time he looks at me.

I see them in his eyes—watching, waiting for me to fail him too.

His heart is locked in a box with no key. His arms outstretched like wings that never landed—no place to rest, no place to call home.

I want to be his peace—he's in pieces.

I try to hold him, press grateful hands into his scalp, whisper safety into his skin. He says he has a headache.

We are intimate with no quality time. He pushes me away with feelings of inadequacy. What did I do?

I question as my eyes burn with resentment. I feel disapproval between the kisses and space between our bare skin. Two hearts racing to see who will finish first.

Neither of us satisfied, I can see him crawl into himself and call it "fun"—

A bed with one side always cold and hands that couldn't feel further from the truth—

He's slipping—not away, but under currents I can't navigate.

He's always been here, yet I have never reached him.

He wanted to be needed—but never believed he was worth being kept.

MUSTANG HEART

My love ran like a mustang—wild, feral, bloodlust in every hoofbeat. It gallops through open fields no map could name, hooves pounding prayers into the dirt.

It cannot be broken by hands that only know how to hold or hurt. Fingertips stained with old blood. Untamed. Untrained. It bonds slowly—a flicker, a flame, a slow burn that either warms you or devours you whole.

It bonds to one soul at a time, a smoldering ache that licks your ribs, sears your lungs, leaving charred flesh you'll never shed.

And yet I belonged to everyone and no one at the same time, admired from a distance, feared up close. You called it beautiful—until it turned toward you.

Unbridled emotions—heading south, a trail of crimson hoofprints staining the dust. A map to nowhere and a compass spinning toward your breaking point.

Solidarity lies trampled beneath my iron-shod desires in the name of love. Independence, the only grass grazed in peace. Here, time fractures —the hush before the collapse. Butterflies and flowers weave mockery among the bones—a love to come, stitched in petals and thorns.

No one warned me love was a carousel of disappointment and forgiveness, a rusty wheel that grinds flesh to freedom's final cry.

I became a show pony—punctured by fight or flight in every whispered argument, my skin scored with barbed wire, my heart a sacrificial pool at the altar of your doubt.

I longed to become a statue—cold iron on a stake, unremarkable, unmoved by your spurs, —too stained to sparkle in your eye.

Decorated and dangerous—a beautiful disaster to some, too much for others who tasted my wildness and recoiled at the bite.

There's nothing this heart wouldn't do to make you happy—to carve you a throne from its own bleeding chest, to lay my entrails at your feet like garlands.

This mustang heart loves without limits—and knowing yours has fences dulls the blade of love itself.

Unconditional love met with conditions is a dream rotting in a petting zoo—hands reaching for tame affection that never comes.

An experience of a lifetime but never permanent —to have and to hold something so wild, knowing you never will.

I galloped till my heart splintered—yours dulls behind the fence you built.

I'M GOOD AT MAKING SOMETHING OUT OF NOTHING

I'm good at making something out of nothing—alchemy in stilettos, turning silence into seduction, turning glances into games you never win.

Good at promises—and breaking them with a smile that tastes like sin. I flick whole situations off my collarbone like ash from a cigarette, call it grace, call it savage, call it "whatever helps you sleep."

Letting things roll? They don't freeze fast enough for me. I like my endings sharp, my beginnings slow.

I'm impatient—but I wait. Momentarily I bloom into something too wild to name. I grow into my convictions, not under them. I bury them deep—before they bury me.

I'm a wildflower with teeth, a Venus flytrap in silk, poison ivy you begged to touch. I've tended myself with dangerous care.

I forge from the iron of your tongue—twisted, heated, bent around my fingers until your words forget who they belonged to.

I've built myself from ash—and baby, I still burn.

I'm good at being bad. In life. In my head. But especially—where it matters.

My lips? Red as your second thoughts. Every kiss? Feels like rain on bare skin—unexpected, unforgiving.

I'm unforgettable. And when you're done with me, you'll come back—you always do.

They never get far before regret starts whispering: "what are you doing?" "you up?"

Wrapped in lust, dressed like care.

Mine. Not yours.

I'm good at goodbyes—no see-you-laters. I like my men definitive. Temporarily, completely mine.

Ready to be devoured. Stuffed with testosterone and a shot of espresso that doesn't know its own strength until it hits you.

My pupils dilate. My teeth ache with want.
    Instinct takes over.

I'm good at making it last—as long as you beg
    me to.

I don't leave when I should. I linger. I learn. I ruin.

I'm the life of the party—and the reason it ends.

A natural disaster in heels, already passing through
    —and baby, you'll feel me long after I'm gone.

LOVE LIKE A FUNERAL

She knew loss—I saw it in her eyes from the start. Eyes like shuttered windows, holding the flicker of a thousand fading candles.

She was a planner, not a hair out of place—picture perfect, like a porcelain doll posed for burial.

She smelled of dying roses and rotting citrus, a sweetness turned sour, her perfume thick as embalming fluid, clinging to my skin like a funeral shroud.

Only at peace while sleeping—and in her casket. A wreath of twigs and black petals hung above her like a dirge in bloom.

A menace in my bed—a life after death with no rest. She was easy to love, hard to forget—like biting into a moldy apple: the skin smooth, the core soft with decay.

I watched her live. I watched her die. Over and over.

Her kisses were like eulogies—each one a final breath, a benediction pressed to my lips. Like she knew.

Another loss. The woman I loved no longer lives.

"Out with the old, in with the new" a phrase tattooed to her lips—I never learned how to let go. A thousand funerals, and I pray this is the last.

We celebrated the life that once was, but I'd rather be six feet under than haunted by the echo of her absence.

I loved her deeper than six feet below—as deep as the ocean, though she never felt the tide.

The wrong person felt so right.

Ungrateful hearts entangled in the threads of my devotion. Always something to say, but never anything worth hearing.

Words like arrows pierced the softest parts of me. Poison dripped from her lips, like it was her native tongue.

Silken skin beneath black lace stockings—I was unworthy of touching. Getting too close was never an option.

She teased me with the key to her heart, dangling it like a promise, knowing she would carry it with her to the grave.

THE DAY I STOPPED COUNTING

Five bruises. Six missed calls. Three days sober.
Five hours slept. It's not that bad—it never is.

I counted the footsteps you took walking away,
measured the seconds absence swallowed
whole. Apologies, breakdowns—twice a day,
like clockwork.

Each tally carved into my wrist felt sacred—tragic
—a language I wrote when words choked in
the throat.

Trembling hands led me into situations without
start or end. Heavy breathing rocked me to
sleep as sheep jumped toward slaughter, one
by one, by one.

Two cracked mirrors. One voicemail I'll never
play. Fourteen hours staring at the ceiling.

I threw out the charts. Burned the journals.
Buried the self-help books that dripped with
truths I wasn't built to hold.

Every chart ended with "try harder." Every book
stopped before the disappointment began.

Journaling taught me honesty—but I wasn't ready for what the monster's ink could name.

Therapy said name the feeling. But what if it answers in a dozen dialects of grief?

I tried to alphabetize the chaos—but it never sat still. It never behaved. It never fit in the grid.

Three discarded notebooks. Seventeen torn pages. Too many systems for one broken map.

I was in love with counting. It gave me purpose. Each "I love you" measured like pills—hoping one would heal, or at least numb the knowing.

Every kiss: a checkbox. Every silence: a missed step. Say it enough, hear it enough, and maybe it's true.

Stay long enough, and maybe I won't leave. We both knew I never would.

Love became a currency I couldn't afford.
Counting became faith I couldn't keep.

Seven "I love you's" Four lies. One truth I couldn't say.

Pain without order. Progress without clarity. Forgiveness without closure.

I counted apologies like rosary beads. None brought peace. The weight of regret measured in milligrams—still toxic.

Zero calls from you. Zero answers. Zero proof I mattered.

So I became a martyr—of learning. Things taught. Things unlearned. If my suffering builds bridges, let me cross alone so someone else doesn't fall.

A stopwatch buried in the soil, blooming with weeds. A rusted relic of ambition I refused to dig up.

One sacrifice. Endless lessons. No need to tally anymore.

I stopped counting the ways I failed to forgive myself. Started listening—to the calm that pulsed like breath, that didn't ask me to perform.

There's freedom in forgetting what kept me caged. There's peace in living outside the record.

I bloom now in unmeasured minutes. I exist where clocks don't tick. I speak in the language of ash and becoming.

I stopped counting. And for once, the silence was mine.

The Day We Finally Saw Each Other

I let a shard of glass slip from my fingers into the rubble at our feet. It cuts the silence—echoing through hallways lined with ashes.

The unspoken looms between us like a question we never learned to ask. Your coat lies on the floor—an abandoned confession in wool. The hush is as heavy as grief.

The sink is half-filled, dishes askew, and the knife waits on the counter—cold, accusatory. The faucet mourns in the quiet, pleading for the shell of our skin to breathe again. Two souls lost in the rubble of what we were.

Outside, rain falls like a curtain slowly parting—each drop a confession neither of us knows how to voice. We feel the wind on our backs but not each other's warmth. The storm washes our voices clean, threatening to erase everything we said.

Tears pool red where rain meets the floor—sacramental water on wounded skin. I press my palm to your bleeding knuckle, baptizing our anger in the same wetness.

God watches from the cracked ceiling, waiting for one of us to forgive first.

We kneel beside broken plates as if before an altar, offering up our shame in jagged confessionals of porcelain.

Slowly, our hands bridge the gap—fingertips grazing bruised skin over scattered glass. In the knife's reflection, our faces tremble, distorted at first, then—becoming clear.

I strike a match and light the candle on the kitchen island. Its glow reveals tear-stained cheeks, steam rising from our cold mugs. That single flame becomes our altar, our small sanctuary where we speak raw truths beneath its halo.

We can't rebuild this house tonight, but we will sit in the doorway together. Two shadows kneeling by the candle—rain still falling outside.

We didn't stitch every wound, didn't mend every hard edge—but we folded our arms around the same light.

We didn't fix it all—but we finally stopped fighting alone.

CHAPTER IV
AFTER THE ASHES

THE SCULPTURE GARDEN

I am the sculptor—I carve from love and terror, hammering hope into marble until it bleeds.

I've shaped her face from stone with veins throbbing like severed arteries, chiseling splinters deep into flesh with every "How I loved you" and "You're just like her," and "If you really loved me, you'd—"

I press cold steel to my son's skin, whispering, "A man can't be soft—I'll make you hard enough to survive." So I chip away his tenderness and watch the light leave his eyes.

I trace my daughter's hair one carved strand at a time, speaking prayers she never asked for: "Stay safe, girls don't need trouble, be grateful he ignores your cries." Her marble scalp cracks with every curse I bless her with.

In my garden of statues—wives, sons, daughters— they stand worshipping my touch, their powdery tears drying on chipped shoulders.

I meant well. Every stroke was "protection." Every cut, a confession of how much I feared losing them. But granite hearts fracture, and bone statues crumble under the weight of good intentions.

In the empty church of my making, I laid offerings of fractured shields—apologies carved in salt and blood. I prayed to a God who whispered through shattered glass, "Hold them. Don't mold them."

But I never learned that craft. So I keep carving, keep chanting my hollow sermons—each "I did this for you" echoing off cold stone.

Now I walk among my sculptures, their vacant eyes accusing me in the hush before dusk. And finally, I understand:

I was born to build—yet everything I touch crumbles to bone.

THE SCULPTOR'S HANDS
(COMPANION)

He meant well. That's what they always say about men who carve with trembling hands and call it love.

He was a sculptor. Not of stone—of people. Of hearts. Of futures. Of women who stayed too long and boys who never learned how to run.

He spoke in chisel strokes. Words sharp enough to shape you, soft enough to make you stay.

He'd say, "I only want to make you better." But *better* always looked *broken*.

He'd chip away at your softness until only silence remained. He'd polish your pain until it gleamed like obedience.

He called it art. But every statue he made cracked from the inside. Every soul he touched turned to dust in his hands.

He didn't know why. Didn't understand how something so carefully crafted could collapse under the weight of his good intentions.

He thought love was a hammer. That healing was subtraction. That to protect meant to reshape.

But he never asked what we wanted to be.

He carved until we no longer looked like ourselves. Until we no longer looked at all.

And when we shattered, he wept—not for us, but for the pieces he couldn't put back together.

He knelt at the altar of his own confusion, offering up our ruins as proof that he tried.

But I saw God watching from the margins. Not in the cathedral, not in the sculptor's studio—but in the dust on the floor.

And I heard Him whisper:

"You were never meant to carve them. You were meant to hold them."

But the sculptor never learned how to hold without shaping. How to love without altering. How to see beauty without "improving" it.

So he keeps carving. Keeps praying. Keeps wondering why everything he touches turns to stone.

And I wonder—how many more will he sculpt before someone breaks the chisel?

THE GOD I GAVE BACK

I was given a god wrapped in stained pages, a
    boxed future buried under rituals. I was gifted
    a god with mirrors for eyes who only saw
    my sin.

They draped him in scripture and called it
    unconditional. I kept him out of obligation,
    tucked beneath my ribs like a blade.

The crucifix on my wall became a restraint. A
    black leash of condemnation chased me down,
    gripped my neck like my faith depended on
    suffering.

A twisted vine of thorns tightened around my
    throat, screaming—"This is what you did
    to me."

The god they gave me hates me. Hates what is evil
    —adores good works. But don't talk about the
    good, or the devil might hear and pride will
    swallow you whole.

Miss one Sunday? "To hell with you!" his followers scream—a choir of zombies chanting truths they wrote in their own image.

They became gods themselves with every breath aimed like bullets in my direction. Held the gavel because they were older, louder, more loved by their version of him.

God nodded along as anvils of doctrine fell on hardened hearts, pounding belief into bone.

If your blood isn't splattered on concrete, if your neurons don't fire scripture they can see—you are unworthy. Unworthy of love. Unworthy of *our* god. You're not one of us. You can join—but you can't leave.

Look at the list of life: You're not living unless you sacrifice.

Crucify your flesh. Skin yourself to the bone. Peel away the parts you love and replace them with their god—because that's what he did for you.

Love must be measured to be real. Conditional. Visible. Painful.

Leave the church—and you leave their god. You leave them.

They chant in circles of salt, forged from their sweat and sacrifice. They place a red hood over my head and call it mercy.

Blood soaks through what I realize is a burial shroud.
"We want you to live—so you must die," they proclaim.

Bible verses fall from their mouths like fists. Every word, every prayer—a command. Each bruise offered in the name of love.

"We don't sit with sinners," they preach—as if their savior died for a mirror.

By grace, I ran.

I handed him back—no prayer, no guilt. Raised my hands as if they held nothing.

I wanted bleach to rinse the blood that didn't feel like mine. Instead, I peeled him off my skin like scripture gone stale.

Returned the weight he left behind. Dropped a god-shaped relic into the earth.

Let flame lick the corners of doctrine. Let my heartbeat un-sync from fear. I did not look back.

I carried the lessons they were too afraid to learn. Took the road they never dared—afraid of the unknown more than the lie.

I searched for truth and stumbled into a cathedral split down the middle: vines strangling one half, fire consuming the other.

I opened the door. Found an altar where my house used to stand—built from breath, bone, and choice.

A closed Bible, bleeding light from its spine, caught my eye.

I met God in the silence I was taught to fear. He didn't look like their instructions. No sermon. No shadow. Just presence: Unmeasured. Unmasked. Enough.

They said, "If you seek truth, you'll find it."

I found peace in that hush—a spark of hope flickering in the ashes of my former self.

I chased Him into the fire, but He waited in the breath I stopped trying to earn.

Let them worship their cages; I choose the flame— the ruthless grace of burning clean.

I'm not just alive—I am living. He doesn't dwell in pages; He burns in me.

EDGE OF INFINITY

They say I have a knack for writing—each word a command that stirs the wind or sparks a flame, blooming like stars across the black sky, constellations burned into my mind.

I search for myself in waves of feeling, from sunlit beaches where foam hisses over bare toes to coral cathedrals in the deep, always hunting for the place I belong.

Footprints in the sand whisper of those who came before—mine press into memory like the final line of an unfinished story, marking a legacy that might never be read.

Between my life and destination hovers a question mark in shifting dunes, decisions tumbling in its curve. Each step trembles with hesitation: "I'm just stopping to smell the roses," I lie, hiding doubt in petals of excuse.

No map guides this lone traveler to home. I vow to marry into the family I choose because the one I was born into cast me out like a fractured stone.

Once battle ready, I stood at the bay's edge in regret-forged armor; now I pry rusted plates from my frame, wade into the surf's icy grasp to face my fury, then slip into a hidden cove of calm and lift a hymn for a war quietly won.

My spoken words become anchors in storms, yet when the sea rages they unfurl to eagle wings, catching stray winds of hope and lifting battered spirits skyward.

There's something sacred in relatability—to spill my grief into open ears and taste understanding on another tongue. I long for a stranger's hand in mine, their fingers echoing my ache—two hearts pulsing in the same vast silence.

Galaxies drift between us—we float like separate stars in skies of our own making, surrounded by light yet unseen.

Mountains blur into mist, peaks we once scaled fading into ghosted ambitions. The only limit I ever knew was myself, chained by judgments I wore like shackles.

Missed chances lie abandoned like broken homes,
> their roofs caved in by calloused pride that
> suffocated hope before it could breathe.

Above me, the sky cracks with silent questions,
> veins of silver lightning stirring existential
> tension. My compass spins inward—seeking
> true north in a world without maps.

I shout into the void—silence answers back in
> starlight, tiny sparks quivering in the black.

Infinity pauses—not empty, but listening—and in
> that breathless moment I find my stride.
> Home is never a place on a map; it is the name
> I give to knowing.

The Clock That Forgot Me

There's a clock that sits in the fireplace. It waits patiently—telling me it's time to go, what's taking so long, why are you always late, why can't you ever be on time?

It beckons. And sometimes, I beckon back.

I watched my worth seep through the cracks of this house. Its hands melted in the fire. I stood in the ash of every deadline I ever worshipped and felt nothing but the wind threading through my ribs.

No more ticking. No more "should have." No more spine bent to the rhythm of someone else's pace.

Healing didn't arrive on schedule. It came limping —mud-caked and feral, with teeth like memory and eyes like mine.

One step forward. Two steps back. It didn't knock. It broke in. Slept in the ruins of my chest and called it home.

It left me broken, then circled back when I found the strength to shower, to wash my hair, to look in the mirror without flinching at the reflection that used to laugh.

A face behind fractured glass tells me what I've become—and what I'll never be. It chains me to my past and calls me free.

My worth went down in flames. For a while, there was nothing left to spark a flame, to light the candle on the table.

And maybe—maybe I didn't want to. Look at the mess I've made. I sit in the soot, trying to remember how I got here, knowing the answer is staring back at me.

I stopped counting. Stopped measuring. Let the days bleed into each other like watercolor bruises. Let the silence stretch until it became a shape I could live in.

Time is a ghost now. It watches from the corners, but it can't touch me. Can't name me. Can't fold me back into the before.

My worth lies beneath the ground. And I went digging for answers.

I am not a recovery arc. Not a neat return. I am the smoke that lingers after the structure fell. I am the breath that refuses to be timed.

The clock forgot me—and in the forgetting, I became:

Not healed. Not whole. But real. Unmeasured. Unfolding. Mine.

Let the ashes keep the time.

WHISPERS OF THE WIND

Off the cliff, the wind comes soaring—a hushed courier of stories, emotions unseen, unheard, brushing past those who never pause to hear.

It kisses the squirrel good morning, lifts the birds toward their dreams, and in the distance, a child's laughter rings as the wind strokes her cheek with a feather borrowed from the sky.

A gentle reminder: go with the flow—let dreams rise like kites in an open field.

Down by the shore, the wind lays a fresh coat of salt on the sunbathers and wave chasers, seasoning their stillness with motion.

To those who chase the sun, it offers cool relief—a breath against scorching skin.

Flags flutter above sandcastles built by hands that dared to believe. Fragile kingdoms, destined to dissolve when left to the tide's forgetting.

Through trees and over hills it rustles, carrying secrets only shadows dare keep.

It bears the scent of meals made with love, the sharp tang of shattered wine bottles, and the soft hush of a new beginning—all drifting across the landscape like a hymn only the wind remembers.

And when it leaves—it takes nothing, yet changes everything.

That's the power of what we never see coming.

WHAT THE RIVER DIDN'T TAKE

I press My palm to her throat—feel her heartbeat quiver under skin.

Have you ever tried to drown your grief?

The river took My childhood laughter, adrift like empty bottles sloshing cold in murky whirlpools.

The shape of my first heartbreak, braided into reeds, washed into fragile driftwood skeletons.

My mother's lullaby—reduced to foam I cannot sing, echo stripped of its melody.

Petal-soft promises, pressed between pages, now petal-soup in the silt.

I press My throat again—her pulse, a distant roar.

The river couldn't take The seed lodged in a crack, green defiance pushing through stone.

The scar on My ankle—a roadmap deeper than any current.

That bone-deep laugh that bubbles up unbidden, splashes across her surface.

My own name, echoing in bedrock, louder than any cascade.

At first, I thought she was eraser, purifier, destroyer—but she is midwife, too.

Under her belly, life hatches: larvae unfurl into wings, fish trace calligraphy of light, algae script emerald poems on wet stone.

Grief is not mere loss—it's fertilizer for new roots.

In return . . . she left me Patience—years of spray carving slate from stone. Resonance—the rapids' hymn humming in My bones. Clarity—pools so still I glimpse sky in My reflection. Communion—I cup her tears in My hands, drinking without drowning.

I cup My palm to her throat—taste salt and sunrise rising in My veins.

She couldn't wash away My roots—because they grow on both banks.

I am riverbed and shoreline—I am loss and bloom.

I am the current—and the bank.

Now when I cup My palm to the river's throat, I feel . . . *She couldn't wash away My roots—* because they grow on both banks.

SYMPHONY OF SHADOWS

I am starving for attention, so I feed on what lingers in the shadows. A lone candle trembles on the rotted windowsill, its flame a fractured heartbeat against the hush, wax weeping molten memories onto my palm—fossilized promises clinging to the last words we spoke.

The hush of floorboards under moonlight echoes in my chest—dust motes dance in the beam of a dying streetlamp, tiny specters swirling like regrets reborn. Silhouettes pulse on cracked plaster walls, each curved edge a confession etched in smoke —"We saw you," they whisper, their voices tripping over one another like racing heartbeats. "You hid behind lies."

Outside, the twilight sky fractures—half bruised purple, half pale regret—turning my reflection into a half-remembered dream, torn between dawn's promise and midnight's scars.

I raise a trembling hand toward the glow, fingers quivering like piano keys before confession, striking chords in this symphony of shadows until every cast silhouette stretches long, mocking my breath.

The flame flinches—my heart pounds, mortar cracks open beneath my ribs, exposing the cavern where my secrets slept—and I watch the shadows recoil, terrified of the light they summoned.

I step into the circle of illumination, cradling that small sun in my shaking palm, and one by one the phantoms dissolve, ashamed to linger where truth burns bright.

In the end, even shadows must face the light.

THREADS OF TIME

I make my bed upon waking—gold threads lace the blanket's edge, pulled tight between dawn's promise and the ache of yesterday's sighs.

Time, the silent weaver, loops birth and loss into every stitch, its shuttle humming beneath my fingertips.

I press my palm to the seams—each filament once pulsing with newness: first breath of friendship, flowering of love, a soul's bright spark. Now they wear the hush that follows the soft crack of dreams unspooling.

In the corner, moth-eaten blankets hang ghosts-like, exhaling centuries of unclaimed grief. Their frayed hems cradle lullabies of loss— choruses that never learned to fade.

Floorboards groan beneath my weight, bearing the footprints of a thousand yesterdays. Dust motes drift as time's fine ash, dancing through shafts of slanted sunlight—tiny sparks of what has been.

I spill my coffee on blueprints of tomorrow I have yet to draw—brown rivulets darkening hopeful plans, ink bleeding promise into worn woodgrain. Each hiss of the kettle echoes the distant clang of future regrets.

My breath becomes the shuttle—each exhale pulling thread through today's living loom, every heartbeat a fresh stitch in the tapestry I shape. Coffee cups clink like lowered caskets, clocks melt into shadows, their hands dripping minutes like candle wax.

Ahead, one golden strand gleams—a slender promise hidden in dusk's hush. I tremble at its glow, caught between fear and longing, daring not yet to unroll its secret.

I tug too hard—the blanket quivers beneath my grasp, and in that single, final yank, the thread snaps.

The world tilts, suspended in the breath of forever—past, present, future woven into one grounded moment.

The thread snaps, and time doesn't move.

WHEN A CITY BREATHES

Before dawn, taillights stream like fire-honed rivers. Each horn blast freezes me—a flake of regret in rush-hour frost. Windows flare ember-red soft as the sun pries open its eyes, a bear lifting its heavy head from granite boughs. A city stretches, a bear rousing from concrete hibernation. Steam rises from subway grates—it's slow exhale beneath concrete fur—promise struck beneath steel skies.

Alarm clocks shake the beds of many. A lone birdsong stirs a canopy, shaking leaves like whispered prayers. Streetlights blink out, stars fading at the edge of morning. A city yawns—steam curling from its nostrils like breath on winter air. It stretches through rusted scaffolding, blinks through traffic lights.

Coffee brews in kitchen dens, bitter and hot as bark peeled from a waking tree. We sip it like ritual, bracing for a hunt. Hungry for money, motivated by food. A pot gurgles—sap rising in spring. Time pauses, then tightens its grip with each tick of a clock.

We spill into streets like startled starlings,
 briefcases clutched like talons, chasing time
 through asphalt rivers. A bear is hungry now
 —its belly growls in subway rumbles, its claws
 scratch the sky in cranes and cables. We are
 foragers, dodging yellow-eyed predators,
 praying a day won't devour us whole.

Crosswalks become migration paths, office
 buildings—hives that never sleep. Primal
 instinct: work or be outworked. People scatter
 like birds wherever sunlight lands. Horns
 crack like ice on winter ponds, steel carcasses
 inch forward—each driver a sandcastle soul
 washed away by lunchtime tides.

Inside glass dens, we hunch over glowing screens,
 decoding a day's demands like ancient runes.
 Some sleep through the sun—night owls
 curled in blackout caves, dreaming of silence
 while a bear prowls above. A city watches
 itself in mirrored windows, unsure if it's
 predator or prey.

We gather at watering holes, routines etched in
 our roots—so familiar we could do them
 blind. New tasks weigh like paperweights in
 hand. Graveyard shift workers blink in
 daylight, traffic herds return to a flock.

As dusk unfurls its bruised tapestry—purple dusk bleeding into molten gold—a bear yawns, its amber roar rolling across rooftops. Cranes rise like herons from marshy scaffolds, and pigeons roost like ghostly doves upon steel limbs. Its breath slows as the sky bruises. We rush home, plastic bags swinging like prey. Kitchens flicker to life—stovetops hiss like snakes in a brush. Some eat saying nothing, others speak in fragments between bites and bills. A day's weight settles like snowfall on shoulders.

Beneath neon vines, strangers' paths converge—whispers shared like roots beneath the surface. With or without purpose, we breathe the same air. Skyscraper windows flare ember-red. Pigeons roost on steel boughs. I rise with them, unshackled, singing hymns for wars I quietly won.

A city curls into itself, its heartbeat slowed to the rhythm of late-night reruns and scrolling thumbs. Loneliness drifts like wind through empty trees. Lovers reconnect—wolves howling across valleys. Phone screens become stars in our palms—stared at, worshipped, absorbing a space between us.

Some whisper into phones like wolves across canyons. Others lie beside lovers, their silence louder than sirens. Spiders spinning webs of whispered connection. Loneliness drifts through alleyways like a lone fox, soft paws padding on moonlit stones. Some murmur through their screens—voices echoing like lost wolves across canyon walls. Others lie side by side in borrowed darkness, their silence deeper than a city's siren song.

A bear dreams—of rivers it once drank from, of forests paved over, of peace it never quite remembers.

And in that hush—a city inhales, steel ribs expanding against the dark—then exhales anew.

THE LIGHT BETWEEN RUINS

I slip my fingertips into yesterday's fire scars—the mortar splits beneath my touch, hollow but humming with old prayers. What led me here, amid charred rafters and skeletal vines, where every fallen beam feels like a confession?

I wander these ash-soft corridors, knees brushing shattered tiles, eyes tracing the skeleton of walls once tall and proud. In a pile of rubble—slick with soot—I discover a single sprout of green; its blade trembling like a first-lit flame.

I cradle it in my palm, feel its pulse sync with my own. Hope tastes like chlorophyll and sunrise, and I vow to build from this promise.

Here, ruin becomes the blueprint for a stronger foundation: I scoop broken brick into my arms, stack them with lessons learned—each charred edge a memory I won't repeat. My mortar is resolve, my scaffold constructed from yesterday's burns.

I press my back against jagged stone—breathe ash and possibility—and plant seeds in every crack.

Between each shattered fragment, I sow new roots: a vine of commitment wrapping through my veins, moss of forgiveness carpeting my feet. Ruin is not my tomb but my cradle, fermenting the nutrients of survival.

With each sunrise, I lift these walls—brick by disciplined brick—until my bones become bedrock and my heart, an altar of resilience.

In this crucible of collapse, I learn to rise: Patience like river-smoothed stones; Resilience humming in marrow; Clarity gleaming in my reflected gaze; Promise cupped in both hands—drinking salt without sinking.

Now, when I cup my palm to the ruin's throat, I taste smoke and seedling green rising in my veins. I will not fall back into old cracks or worship fragile towers of false hope.

Between these ruins, I become the architect of my becoming—loss transformed to bloom, ashes reformed to ember.

I am the light that roots in rubble, the promise that refuses to break.

REFLECTIONS

CHAPTER I: A SINGLE EMBER

This was the ache before the scream. I wrote these poems with trembling hands, hoping someone might hear the quiet desperation beneath my held-in emotions.

Every line was a flicker—grief trying to name itself, longing trying to survive.

I didn't know if I was worthy of love, but I knew I needed it. This chapter includes the embers I carried in my chest when everything else felt cold.

Yes, it's a glimmer of hope. But it's also a reminder of what's left of my held-back self.

I look around and see the wreckage—the flame they tried so hard to stomp out. The sacrifices I made cost me more than my spark.

A single ember is what remains of me on some days. And on others, my fire consumes everything in my path.

This is the beginning of the end. And the end of who I used to be.

CHAPTER 11: THIS IS WHERE I BURN

Here is where I stopped apologizing. I let the fire speak. I let the rage rise.

These poems are not polite—they are sacred rebellion.

I confronted *the gods I was told to worship*, the lovers who mistook my softness for surrender. I let the nest burn —because it was never safe.

This fire was started by others: their arrows, their betrayals, their vengeful silences.

And yes, I was sad when it all went down in flames. But it was there, in the wreckage, that I learned to dance in the blaze. To move with the heat. To become free fire.

This chapter is my ignition point—holy, furious, and free.

CHAPTER III: SMOKE SIGNALS

After the fire, I wandered through the smoke. These poems are maps made of memory—symbols rising from ash, truths whispered through haze.

I searched for meaning in the aftermath, for connection in the quiet. I didn't always find answers, but I found echoes.

This chapter is the dreamscape of survival—soft, surreal, and still smoldering.

Once I came to the end of my old self, and the smoke cleared, I found God. Not in the church I left behind, but in the relationship I'd been searching for—without conditions, without blood contracts.

I am still emotional. Still an empath. Still someone who feels everything deeply—even when I wish I didn't.

Emotions are not my guiding light anymore, but they still live in me. I'm learning to move with intention, to choose stillness over reaction, reason over rupture.

It's difficult. Some days I fail. But I'm putting in the work to become who I'm meant to be—not just who the pain shaped-shifted me into.

I still have more questions than answers most days. Some days, poetry feels like a walk in the forest. Other days, the tree line becomes a prison.

If you spend too much time off the trail, you will get lost. But sometimes, getting lost is the only way to be found.

CHAPTER IV: AFTER THE ASHES

I built an altar from ruin. These poems are not about healing—they are about honoring what remains.

I found grace in the rubble, light in the cracks, and a kind of peace that doesn't promise perfection.

I am still a phoenix in progress, but I no longer fear the ash. This chapter is my offering—rooted, luminous, and sacred.

I am still not healed, but I am human. A condition I know well—and some days, I forget.

There are moments I wish I didn't carry so much knowing, didn't earn my wisdom through wounds. But here I am.

This altar is no longer for worshipping. It's for visiting. When I need to come home—to who I am.

I'm learning balance, though I've yet to master it. Some days I rise. Some days I rest in the ash. Both are sacred. Both are mine.

ACKNOWLEDGMENTS

To my publisher, cover designer, and editor—thank you for your patience as I reshaped this vision, again and again, until it felt true. You honored the process, not just the product. You saw the spark and helped it rise. Even when the flame flickered and the vision shifted, you stayed. You breathed life into this book—into every page, every bone, every ember. It carries your fingerprints, your faith, and your craft.

To my friends and family—I know I was not always easy to walk beside. I became the storm, the silence, the sharp edge. But you stayed. You loved me in the dark and the fire. You taught me that love doesn't need perfection —it just needs presence.

To the ones who left—who couldn't hold the weight of my love, though I carried yours with open hands and an unguarded heart. You taught me the sacred art of letting go.

To every reader who finds part of themselves in these pages—thank you. You are not alone.

ABOUT THE AUTHOR

Melaine Harvey is a poet, visual storyteller, and founder of *AnthroPoetica* and *Pyre & Petals Press*. Her work rises from rage, grace, and sacred survival—unapologetic, visceral, and hauntingly beautiful. Born in Denver and raised in Pueblo, Colorado, she now creates from Woodbridge, Virginia, where high plains, red earth, and urban edges shape her imagery.

Her poetry is a reckoning and a sanctuary—written for the ones who feel too much and say too little, for the ones who flinch at love but still hope. She turns pain into flame, crafting elemental language that speaks of feathers, embers, and the sacred ache of transformation.

Rooted in divine truth and emotional honesty, Melaine's work reflects a faith that transcends religion. Her imprint, *Pyre & Petals Press*, is a sanctuary for art that burns with purpose and rises in grace. She believes in the holiness of imperfection, the beauty of survival, and the radical grace of being unapologetically oneself.

Melaine's creative process is raw and relentless. She writes, rewrites, and sits with the ache until it tells the truth. Her poems aren't polished—they're lived. They carry bruises, bite marks, and the kind of silence that eventually screams. She believes in survival as art, in beauty that bleeds, and in the power of saying the thing no one wants to say.

Her mission is fierce and unwavering: to be the voice she needed when everything was too loud, when the pressure and pain were too much to hold. To speak into the moments when she broke and felt utterly alone. When heaviness became a person—and he wanted her dead. Her work doesn't promise healing. It promises honesty. And sometimes, that's the only thing that saves us.

She is a phoenix in progress. A firekeeper with dirty hands. A truth-teller who writes to feel, to heal, and to burn clean.

www.ingramcontent.com/pod-product-compliance
Lightning Source LLC
LaVergne TN
LVHW011420080426
835512LV00005B/166